Donna Watson and her mother, Norma Church

DEDICATION

*To a beautiful lady
who is more than my mother.
She is also
my friend.*

101 WAYS TO ENJOY LIFE'S *Simple* PLEASURES

Donna Watson, Ph.D.

Author of
101 SIMPLE WAYS TO BE GOOD TO YOURSELF

Bard & Stephen

AUSTIN, TEXAS

For information about quantity purchases contact:

Bard & Stephen
5275 McCormick Mountain Drive
Austin, Texas 78734
512-266-2112 Phone
512-266-2749 Fax

Paperback edition: ISBN 1-885167-00-8

Hardcover edition: ISBN 1-885167-01-6

Bard &
Stephen
AUSTIN, TEXAS

Copyediting: **Helen Hyams**
Proofreading: **Debra Costenbader**
Text Design: **Suzanne Pustejovsky**
Jacket/Cover Design: **Suzanne Pustejovsky**
Composition/Production: **Round Rock Graphics**

CONTENTS

◇

THE AUTHOR

Donna Watson is a high-energy, internationally known speaker who has taught at every level from preschool through college, directed a direct-sales company, hosted a radio talk show, and done training for Fortune 500 companies. Presently she owns her own consulting company, working predominantly in the area of stress management. She is also the president of U R Special Ministries, Inc., a nonprofit corporation that helps at-risk children, and she and her husband, Robert, are marketing directors in a pharmaceutical company.

Her MBA and Ph.D. degrees in management and twenty-five-year career in training and motivational speaking have given her a wealth of knowledge that she uses to successfully coordinate her varied personal and professional interests.

Donna's favorite professional pastime is sharing practical, life-enriching ideas in a commonsense and inspirational manner. Since her husband's retirement, she and Robert enjoy traveling and sharing those ideas with others in person and through radio and television appearances.

When she can sneak in personal time, Donna loves to spend it with her family and friends and to write, sew, and paint.

◇

INTRODUCTION

Isn't it amazing how the simple things in life so often end up being the most important? Just think about the things that bring joy and meaning to your life every day.

High on your list might be a hug from someone special or laughing with a friend. Maybe it's a beautiful sunrise, the smell of baking bread, browsing in a used book store, or just taking a walk that puts things back into perspective.

You see, life is a combination. It is big events and actions and little incidents and deeds. So often it is the little things that count the most. These "simple pleasures" make life worthwhile and help us thrive.

Your special simple pleasures will not be the same as mine, but maybe you'll be inspired to try something new or to rediscover some long-forgotten source of happiness.

Here's to your simple pleasures. Please don't ever become so involved with the big things in life that you miss out on them.

God bless you,

*Teach us delight in
simple things.*

—RUDYARD KIPLING

BEST FRIENDS

*B*est friends can pick up a conversation with you when you haven't been together in years.

Best friends can finish your sentences because they know you well enough to know how you feel.

Best friends are the people you can call at three o'clock in the morning, long-distance, and say "I'm hurting" or "I'm excited," and they understand.

Best friends will support you even though they don't understand.

Best friends are the people who share our greatest triumphs and our simple pleasures.

Best friends are one of the greatest joys in life.

MOONLIT NIGHTS

I love to wake up on a night when the moon is full and look at the world around me in the moonlight. It has such a special glow. The shadows are richer and fuller, enhanced by the moonlight.

Being away from the city makes you appreciate the beauty of the night even more. When I can escape from the lights, I like to take a late-night drive and just look at the stars, the clouds, and the shape of the moon.

Do you remember stargazing when you were a child and locating the Big Dipper or the North Star? Maybe it is time to try it again. Don't miss the pleasure of the night's natural beauty.

LISTEN TO THE RAINDROPS

*L*isten. It is raining. Can you hear the raindrops hitting the roof? Look at the window. The patterns the rain makes as it runs down the pane have always fascinated me.

There is something very peaceful about rain. It makes me want to curl up in bed or in front of a big roaring fire in the fireplace and read a good book.

A nice slow rain is peaceful and calming. It says, "Slow down. Take it easy. We have time."

4

GRANDDAD'S
VEGETABLE GARDEN

*M*y granddad raised a vegetable garden, all by himself, until he was ninety-eight. He tilled it with an old-fashioned, hand-pushed plow, and it was his great joy in life. He not only loved to work with the earth; he enjoyed eating the fresh vegetables, raw as well as cooked.

When I was a little girl, I used to go over to his house and work in the garden with him. I adored being with him and doing anything he did.

Grandma was a great cook and always fixed huge meals. She would spend the whole morning in the kitchen cooking up a fabulous meal, and Granddad and I would spend it in the vegetable garden, tasting the wonderful raw vegetables. By noon, I was interested in almost anything except lunch. That's when the trouble would start. Grandma would ask me, "How could you eat all those raw vegetables and ruin your lunch?" and then she'd accuse my grandfather: "How could you allow her to do that?" Granddad and I were always in trouble. We would just look at each other, shrug our shoulders, and do it again.

As Francis Bacon said, "God Almighty first planted a garden. And, indeed, it is the purest of human pleasures." For my granddad, it was.

Here's to you, Granddad. You were the love of my life.

PUTTER

*D*o you ever just "putter"? It is one of those old-fashioned words we don't see around much anymore, like "icebox" and "parlor."

Perhaps the word has disappeared because we have forgotten how to putter. We used to putter in the kitchen and bake a cake or some cookies, just for fun. But now, many of us have forgotten how to putter in the kitchen or the garage, or we may not even have a garage anymore.

Has the hustle-bustle life we are so engrossed in taught us that puttering is a waste of time? Well, it isn't. Maybe life wouldn't be so hectic if we puttered once in a while.

PUPPY LOVE

*O*ne day, on my morning walk, I discovered a little black ball of fur on the grass. She jumped up, shook herself, and ran straight for me, so I took her home for one night until I could decide what to do with her.

Ten years later Teddy Bear was still with us, winning the hearts of everyone she met. She was always at the door when we came home. She would get so excited that her whole body would shake, not only her tail. She always listened when we needed to talk. She never criticized. She never complained. She just loved us.

Teddy Bear is gone now, but she will always be one of the great pleasures of our lives. No one ever told her she was a dog. She just thought she was a part of the family.

SLEEPING IN

How long has it been since you took a whole morning to do exactly what you wanted?

Think about it for a moment. What would you do with that morning? Would you sleep in late? How about breakfast in bed? You might take time to read the newspaper or maybe watch an old movie on TV. How about cuddling up to someone special for a little private time together?

We rush through life, running from one appointment to another, even when the appointment is for golf or tennis. We forget the great pleasure in simply slowing down.

Take a morning off. Do whatever you want with it. Sleep late. Read a good book. Work in your garden. Go walking. Make time for yourself. You are special.

8

A JOB WELL DONE

When my daughter left our home, I didn't know whether we would ever share our lives again, and my heart broke.

I cleaned the windows inside and out. I had to make at least one thing better in my life, even if it was only the way the windows looked.

At times like these, it helps to simply do our best at something—even if it is just cleaning windows till they sparkle, polishing furniture to a shine, or cleaning out a closet. We all feel as if we've blown it sometimes. That's when we need to do something that we know we can do well. It restores us. The sense of pride becomes a little pleasure.

9

WALKING IN THE RAIN

*O*ne afternoon in New England Robert and I were taking an extremely interesting walking tour when it started to rain. We looked at each other and I said, "Let's go for it." Why should a little rain ruin our tour?

It drizzled most of the afternoon and we got soaked, but what a memory! We walked, held hands, read the historical signs, climbed the old stone walls, and had a wonderful time.

Certain days always stand out in your memory, and that is one of them for me. New England and the rain.

Sometimes we are so careful with life that we miss its joys. Take a risk. You might miss life!

A SPECIAL GIFT

*T*he Christmas before I lost my dad, I noticed that he was wearing a topcoat he had bought during World War II. I said, "Dad, you need a new topcoat." He protested, but my intuition said that I should buy him an early Christmas present for the following year, so I went out and bought him a new coat.

You should have seen him as he modeled it. Big tears came to his eyes and he said, "I don't deserve anything this nice." But he did.

When Christmas came that year and my dad wasn't there, I was so glad I had listened to my intuition. I didn't have to leave him out. I had already given him his present, and I could still remember the joy on his face and in his eyes.

Listen to your intuition. Know when to buy that special gift. It feels so good inside.

FAVORITE CHILDHOOD BOOKS

*H*ow long has it been since you sat and read a children's book, or walked through the children's section of a wonderful bookstore, or read a story aloud to see the wonder in a child's eyes?

If you can't say "recently," you are missing some of life's greatest pleasures. Stories are not just for children. They allow the child in all of us to run away into a wonderful world of fantasy.

Dig through your attic or garage, find some of your favorite old books, and reread them. Browse through a bookstore or a library—the titles will pop out at you. Maybe you could volunteer your time at the library for a reading session with children. I promise, you will get as much or more pleasure from that time as the children do.

12

BACK PORCH

When I get completely stressed out and exhausted, I don't want to sleep. I want to "do nothing."

One of my favorite places to do nothing is in the lounge chair on my back porch. I can sit in that chair in a rainstorm and feel as if I am in the middle of the storm without getting wet. I can sit there in the heat of summer and read without getting a sunburn. I can lean back, look at the sky and the trees, watch the squirrels, and pretend that I am anywhere in the world. I can escape.

When I have finished doing nothing, I feel ready for anything. What do you do when you do nothing?

13

THE BEACH

*H*ave you ever gone to the seashore and just walked? You had no purpose, no goal. You just walked. You felt at peace, free from everyday cares.

Maybe you are a long way from the ocean. Go there in your mind. Close your eyes for a moment and walk along the beach. Can you hear the waves rolling in and crashing against rocks on the shore? Feel the warm sand on your feet. It's not too hot. It's not too cold. It just feels good.

Now stop for a moment. Sit down. Let the tide drift over your feet and legs. Let the sand sift through your fingers. Listen to the peace and quiet. Get lost in the wonderful sounds of peace. The pleasure is all yours.

A LONG, HOT SOAK

*T*here is something very special about a long, hot soak. Think about a bubble bath. When you sink deep into that warm, bubbly water, all the cares of the world seem to float away. Hot tubs and whirlpool baths are other relaxing ways of totally restoring ourselves.

When I arrive home after an extended business trip, I'm usually exhausted for the first day or so. One of my favorite memories is of the night I came home from a long speaking tour to find a warm bubble bath, prepared by my husband, waiting for my tired and aching body.

Now that is love.

SOLITUDE

*M*y mother is a people person. She wants people around her all the time. She likes to talk with them and listen to them. She needs constant interaction.

Me, I like solitude. Don't get me wrong. I love people and I love to be around them, but sometimes what I want most of all is just peace and quiet.

I don't have to be alone to enjoy solitude. In fact, some of the loveliest moments of peace and quiet that I remember have been spent with my husband. Robert and I can sit and read, or ride and enjoy the sights for hours without talking, just being together. We have the inner peace that comes from knowing that we belong.

Solitude and peace. Sometimes they are synonymous.

MUSIC

*T*urn that noise down!" How often did I yell that when the kids were growing up? And yet, what was noise to me was music to them.

I thought, "How can they stand that racket?" but if I remember carefully, I can hear the echo of those same words from my past. Times change, the tempo changes, our tastes change—but the pleasure of music remains the same.

A LIFE OF GIVING

*W*inston Churchill said, "We make a living by what we get. We make a life by what we give."

What have you given to life lately? Have you given someone your smile? Have you shared your laughter? How about a hug?

Have you paid someone a compliment lately? Have you told a friend how special he or she is? Have you listened with your eyes and your ears?

Have you been there for someone who was hurting? Did you go out of your way just to be kind? Were you willing to share your time and your life?

People should be cherished. When you pass up that opportunity, you pass up life. Giving to people is what life is all about.

ON AN IMPULSE

Are you impulsive? A well-planned life avoids stress and confusion, but unless you give in to impulses from time to time, you will miss many of life's little pleasures.

My family has always been impulsive. I remember the night my daughter and I spent two hours trying to find the source of a searchlight flashing across the city. We often run out for waffles or ice cream at midnight, simply because we are hungry.

Some of the best trips we have ever made were those where we just packed, headed in any direction, and did whatever seemed especially enjoyable at the moment.

We "have" to do so many things to keep life going that it can become boring unless we add in a little fun along the way. Do something impulsive today!

MAKE IT WORK

Sometimes, great pleasure comes from finding a creative way to overcome adversity.

Years ago, I rebuilt a historic home while I was living in it. My mom and dad were wonderful and came up to help me every chance they had. On one of those occasions, it suddenly occurred to us that it was Thanksgiving.

There was no way we could ever make it through all the construction to put together a traditional Thanksgiving dinner. However, I have been blessed with very positive people in my life. We put our heads together and designed one of the most unique and memorable Thanksgiving feasts I have ever shared.

We found some frozen chickens in the freezer. Mom located the electric skillet, some vegetables, and a long extension cord, and she creatively turned the laundry room into what seemed like a gourmet kitchen.

What a wonderful holiday. What could be better? We had good food, a warm home, family, and, yes, even guests.

GOOD DEALS

I am a bargain hunter and take great pleasure in finding good values. We bargain hunters are everywhere. We delight in buying cars, clothes, houses, and groceries at a discount.

It's not only a matter of pride to look around for a special bargain; it's also great fun. It becomes a challenge of wits that both you and the seller can enjoy.

Whether you merely save grocery coupons, buy clothes at off-price outlet stores, or negotiate million-dollar real estate deals, have a little fun. Bargain a little. What have you got to lose? After all, you can always pay full price.

FORGET YOUR WATCH

*H*ave you ever spent an entire weekend without wearing your watch? What about just one afternoon or evening? See? The world didn't come to an end.

Most of us are conditioned to live by our watches. But have you ever seen the daffodils check their watches to know when to bloom? Have you ever seen a bird flying around with a watch? Yet birds seem to know when to eat and sleep, and when to fly south to stay warm for the winter.

Maybe we should take a lesson from nature. Put away your watch for a while and get in tune with life.

A CHILD'S LOVE

*M*y grandson is the greatest joy in my life. When I hold my fingers close together and ask, "Do I love you this much?" he says, "No, MeMe" (that's his name for me), and throwing his arms wide open, he shouts, "You love me all the way to the sky and back!"

It's amazing what wide-open arms and a precious little voice yelling, "Sky, MeMe, sky!" can do for the heart. Children have an incredible ability to love unconditionally. They don't care what we look like, or what we've done, or who we are. They just love.

Do you need someone to love? Join the Big Sister/Big Brother program. Volunteer at a school. Sponsor a Scout group, or just share the love of a friend's child. Children never run out of love. They will always have some for you.

Fly a Kite

I never learned how to fly a kite when I was a kid. So, on my birthday a few years ago, when a friend asked me what I would like, I told her I would like a kite. She took me to a fabulous store full of kites. I had no idea there were so many different kinds.

I chose a simple kite, like the ones I had seen as a child, and for my birthday, my husband took me to the park, helped me attach a tail and a long string to the kite, and taught me how to run until the kite took off on the wings of the air. It was magnificent. It flew effortlessly through the sky as I stood there in awe.

Is there something you have always wanted to do? Why not do it now?

GARAGE SALES

*I*t's been said that one person's junk is another's treasure. That is what garage sales are all about.

In the early days of putting our home together, garage sales were a godsend. They not only helped to furnish our house, but they also stimulated me into very creative decorating. And they were a blessing when we had our children. Children's clothes are outgrown much faster than they wear out, and garage sales are one way to survive on a tight budget.

I still love to go to garage sales, just for fun. It always fascinates me to see what people are buying.

What do you have lying around that just might be someone else's treasure? Have a garage sale and find out.

LISTEN TO THE BIRDS

One of my favorite times of the day is very early in the morning when I go walking through my neighborhood.

I use this time for listening to the birds and thinking. If I am upset with someone I can tell it to the birds and no one gets hurt. If I need to process an idea, I can tell it to the birds and they sing back so beautifully that it makes things seem okay.

Have you ever noticed that birds always seem happy? They sing no matter what is going on in their lives. Maybe we should take a lesson from them. Maybe we should sing more and cry less. You think you can't sing? Sure you can. Everyone can sing in the shower.

26

GOOD SMELLS

*H*ave you ever walked into a home where fresh bread was baking? You can still smell it, can't you? How about the aroma of cookies? My favorite kind is chocolate chip.

When I first went away to school, one of my fondest memories was the way our house smelled when I came home and Mom was fixing my favorite meal.

Other smells are special, too, like the perfume or cologne that lingers when that special someone has left the room.

It's fun what little things give us such great pleasure.

TREE HOUSE

The library in our local elementary school has a tree house right in the middle of the room. It is a big wooden frame that the kids can climb, topped with a platform filled with huge pillows so the kids can get comfy and read. What a great idea!

A friend and I saw this tree house and she said, "Someday I am going to have a tree house that I can escape into." I agreed. We all need tree houses, whether they are an actual structure in the yard or just a corner of the bedroom.

Our tree houses are personal and private and special. They are where we go when we feel as if the world is too hard and we need some extra nurturing. They are our little corner of the world where we create peace and comfort and happiness for ourselves.

Do you have a tree house? Maybe you should.

PLAY

*L*ast week, I took my grandson to the Firefighters' Museum and we crawled all over the fire trucks. We could see the whole city from high on top. We rang the bells, climbed the ladders, and set off alarms. We pretended. I had almost forgotten how to pretend the way a child pretends.

Don't lose your ability to play. Borrow a child if you don't have one handy, and learn how to play again. Children can show you how to make buildings and chairs and people out of blocks. They'll remind you that you don't have to know how to throw a ball to have fun with one and that taking a bath is for more than just getting clean.

Let a child show you how to play.

COUNTRY ROADS

For the past five years, I have traveled extensively on speaking tours, spending most of the day indoors.

When I go home, I often suggest to my husband that we go driving. "Where?" he will usually ask. My reply is "I don't care, let's just drive."

We have found the most interesting little country roads. We didn't know they were there; you can't see them from the freeway. But the little houses tucked back in the trees carry such charm. I always wonder how people found these out-of-the-way places to live. Maybe they were out driving, too. Maybe they decided to make their momentary pleasure permanent. Maybe they were wise.

LIVE IN YOUR SEASON

*E*verything has its
time and its place.
We can't do everything at once.
Maybe some things shouldn't be
done right now. This may not
be the right time.

I see young men and
women graduating from college,
getting a job, getting married,
moving, buying a home, and
having a baby all at the same
time. Then they wonder why
they are stressed out.

We have seasons to our
lives. Just because this isn't your
season to learn how to play the
piano doesn't mean that you
won't ever learn.

Stop for a minute. What
season are you in right now?
Savor it.

A LITTLE
SOMETHING SPECIAL

*W*e so often forget
that fun does not
have to take a great deal of time
or cost a lot of money. It may
be something as simple as
splurging on that special ice
cream cone. Real ice cream—
not that fat-free stuff. Or maybe
relishing a rich, creamy piece
of chocolate that is probably
immoral and certainly fattening,
even if it isn't exactly illegal.

You are very special. You
deserve the best. Give yourself a
little something special.

RENEW FRIENDSHIPS

I had not seen her for a very long time. I didn't know that her son had died. I didn't know that she had started a new business and how well it was doing. I didn't know that she had moved.

We stood and talked for some time and finally wandered into a nearby restaurant and had a wonderful lunch—as good friends do. It was very special, as is she.

As we parted, we pledged to stay in touch. We may, we may not. That doesn't matter. She is my friend and friends can lose touch and still be friends.

What a pleasure that is.

LAUGH OUT LOUD

*W*hen you stop and look, you may notice that we are pretty funny people. We do some dumb things and actually they can be quite funny. One of the greatest pleasures of life is to be able to laugh at ourselves. We need to let others enjoy our antics with us. We need to get in touch with our humor. We need to laugh out loud.

Have a little fun. If you fall down, laugh. If you say something dumb, laugh.

A poem by Ella Wheeler Wilcox reminds us: "Laugh, and the world laughs with you; weep, and you weep alone." I don't know about you, but I would rather have the whole world with me.

HOLDING HANDS

I saw them holding hands. Their eyes met. They smiled and then they laughed together.

KEEP SOME TRADITIONS

*T*he first Christmas after we lost my dad was tough. He had been such a large part of our family and our traditions. In order to survive, we wisely started new traditions. We made new memories and began to build new traditions.

I also found out that you have to keep some of the old rituals. I generally decorate every nook and cranny of our home because I love the holidays. That year I did the basics but that was all. I didn't think anyone would notice.

No one said anything until the holidays were over. Then my daughter said, "There surely were a lot of decorations missing for the holidays, Mom."

New traditions are good, but so are some of the old ones.

TASTE SENSATIONS

*C*an you think of a lemon and make your mouth pucker? How about a pickle?

Isn't it fun to experience life? It is so full of wonderful things. Like a big piece of chocolate cake or a tall, cold soda or a fresh strawberry.

I don't know about you but I'm hungry. I think I'll raid the refrigerator. See you . . .

BOOK BROWSING

*T*he next time you can steal a few minutes from your day, stop by your local bookstore or library and just browse. Browsing is so much fun.

Book titles are the most important part of a book, because that is what we look at when we browse. We see an interesting title and then we stop to look inside.

I also like to browse through personal libraries. You can learn so much about people by looking at what they read.

Browsing is one of my hobbies and, of course, one of my great pleasures in life. You may find that you enjoy it, too.

GO TO GRANDMA'S

*G*randmothers are special. They are not as busy as mothers. They always have time to read a book with you or build a castle with blocks or just listen. Grandmothers are there to make a child's world a little more pleasurable and to build good memories for grown-ups. They are God's way of reminding us that we don't need big, expensive things in our lives to make the world a wonderful place. Sometimes the best times in life come when we are sitting in a grandmother's lap and being hugged.

When you give away a lot of love, you usually get a lot in return. That's what grandmothers do. They love.

REALLY LISTENING

A friend said, "Hi, how are you feeling?" I answered, "Great! How are you feeling?" She replied, "Fine. And now that we're both through lying, how are you *really* doing?"

Really listening is the greatest honor you can pay to someone you care about. It says, "You are special and I care enough about you to give you my undivided attention."

Honor someone today. Listen to them with your eyes and your ears. What a pleasure.

FANTASIZE

*F*antasizing is not a waste of time. By focusing your fantasies, you can accomplish your goals, restore your energy, and give perspective to your life.

Suppose you are having a very bad day. Sit back and close your eyes, and imagine that you can do no wrong. Or remember the time when you said or did something that was just right without thinking about it.

Whoever you are, you do some things right. Don't let anyone tell you differently. No one can read your mind. No one can see the beauty you may have hidden away. No one can see the caring you may have forgotten to show. But it is still there.

Fantasize about the person you would like to become. You can, you know. You are in charge of who you are.

MEALS WITH FRIENDS

*M*ost people enjoy going out to dinner with friends or having them over for a good meal. Some get together to prepare fancy dinners or try out new recipes. Potluck dinners and even sharing carry-out food can be a wonderful excuse to be with friends.

The best part always seems to come after the meal, when we can sit back and really visit. The conversation during the meal seems to be a little pre-liminary—we have to catch up on what the others have been doing. But after the meal, it's different. That is when we get into ideas and thoughts and feelings. That is when friend-ships flourish.

MAKE MEMORIES TODAY

I love the poem by Jenny Joseph that starts "When I am an old woman I shall wear purple." I want to wear purple, and red, and wine, and black, and I want to keep learning.

I never want to stop exploring new and exciting ideas and putting them into action. I want to write and paint and share time with my friends. To travel more, listen more, and talk less. I want to be unafraid to speak my convictions—not in order to impose them on others, but to express who I am.

Someday I want to sit on the front porch and smile and know that I never quit trying and never stopped growing. And I'll know, as I do now, that life's greatest pleasures are what I experience each day.

PICNIC

*D*id you ever go on picnics as a child? On ours, we always had fried chicken and potato salad. We'd play games, then lie on a blanket and watch the birds and the sky. We could take a nap whenever we felt like it. No one said, "We've got to hurry" or "Eat fast, we only have fifteen more minutes." Sometimes we stayed after dark and caught fireflies in a jar. Picnics were stress-free times spent with my family and friends.

Have a picnic. If you're too busy to go somewhere else, how about having one in your backyard? Is it too cold? Use your living room.

QUIET CELEBRATIONS

*T*ake the time to celebrate the good things in your life and the good things you have accomplished.

Stop periodically and remind yourself what you have done well—you finished the contract on time, you soothed a customer's raw nerves, you kissed away some tears, you were there for a friend. Sure, the day wasn't perfect, but it probably wasn't all bad either.

Make a list of accomplishments before you go to bed at night. Even if nothing on your To-Do list got done, think about how you did spend your time. See, you accomplished a great deal. Give yourself a little praise and recognition. You deserve it.

THE CABIN

*W*hen the kids were little, we bought a cabin at the lake. It wasn't fancy, but it was a wonderful, fun place to be.

The cabin had no telephone, no mailbox, no fax machine, and only one TV channel, which didn't always work. The kids could run and play and be safe. I could sit and read, or sleep and relax. The cabin was peaceful and quiet. It was my heaven.

Whether it is a cabin or simply a place in our mind, we all need a safe haven where we can put ourselves back together again, a place that is ours.

46

ANTICIPATE

*W*hich is more fun, having a good time or planning it? Anticipation is at least half the fun.

Think about an upcoming visit with friends or a birthday celebration. Where are you going to be? What special news do you have to share?

Planning and thinking about an activity frequently lasts a lot longer than the activity itself. When someone you love calls in the morning to suggest an evening out, you anticipate it all day, even though the evening itself may last only a few hours.

Look for the good things in your future and anticipate happiness.

STROLL AND SMELL THE FLOWERS

A few years ago, I decided that I must have a better exercise program, so I started walking every day. But at that time I was quite a perfectionist, so I didn't just walk—I kept records. I found that using a certain type of shoe in a certain kind of weather let me walk farther and faster and thus spend less time walking.

Here I was, walking to relieve my stress, and I was creating more stress. When I realized what I was doing, I threw away the charts and started walking according to the dictates of my body. Some days I still walk aerobically, but on others, I just stroll and smell the flowers. To tell the truth, I'm not sure which one is more beneficial.

A SNOWMAN

*A*na was from Mexico. She had never seen snow. Chiques (as we called her) was an exchange student in our home one wonderful year, and she and a young Oklahoma boy enjoyed a special romance during that time.

When the first snow of the winter came and she excitedly ran down the stairs early the next morning, she not only saw her first snow; she also saw her first snowman. Her true love had come to our home in the middle of the night and built it for her.

It's fun to be a kid again. Next winter, put on your scarf and coat and hat and gloves and build a snowman. Use some raisins for his eyes and a carrot for his mouth; give him an old perky hat and let him become a part of your memories.

BIRTHDAYS

I love birthdays. I keep track of hundreds of birthdays of people I know and care about and send birthday cards to several hundred people a year . . . enough so that I even design my own cards.

Throw a party. Celebrate someone's birthday this week. At least one person you know will have one soon or has had one recently. If not, pick a day and celebrate the birthday of someone you don't know—a famous writer, a sports figure, or just someone you admire.

A DIFFERENT PATH

*D*o you always put your left shoe on first? Listen to the same radio station? Eat at the same time and the same place every day? Are you in a rut?

It is so easy to not make a decision. If we just do it the same old way, we won't have to think about it.

What are you missing? New tastes? New sights? New feelings? Are you missing life?

Let me challenge you. Go home by a different route tonight. Get up an hour earlier tomorrow. Go someplace for lunch that you have never been. Eat outside. Call someone in the middle of the day to just say "I love you."

Habits make us unaware. Sharpen your sense of awareness. Don't miss out on life's simple pleasures.

GETTING LOST

I love to paint. One of the reasons I don't paint more often is that I enjoy it so much. I don't want to stop.

When I paint I get lost. My work goes directly from my eyes out through my hand. It is as though my brain is bypassed and can take a rest. Of course, this is the very reason why I should paint more frequently.

Look for something in life that you can put your whole self into—paint, write, read, sew, plant. Getting lost is wonderful. When you can find something that engrossing, don't lose it.

DIAMONDS IN OUR OWN BACKYARD

*R*ussell Conwell wrote a wonderful little book called *Acres of Diamonds*. It was based on a speech he gave over five thousand times. If you have not read it, do yourself a favor.

We all have diamonds in our own backyard. We may have a day when we really need a friend and we think, "I need to find someone who will really be a friend to me right now. I'll look around to see who I can find."

Uh uh. That usually is not the answer. The best friends we have are usually right where we are . . . in our own backyard. Sometimes they are so close we miss them.

REWARDS

*W*hen something must be done and you just don't feel like doing it, set up a reward system for yourself.

Promise yourself a new dress or a new suit when you lose the ten pounds you are working on. Promise yourself a new big-screen TV if you earn that bonus this year. Take a day off to play golf when you finish your taxes.

Remember that it is important to our subconscious mind to keep our promises. What if you've promised yourself the big-screen TV, but when your bonus check arrives you need a new transmission for your car? Buy the TV. If you had not received the bonus, you would still manage to get the car fixed somehow. If you don't follow through, the next time you promise yourself a reward, your subconscious support system will probably say, "Why should I help? The reward won't be there anyway."

We deserve rewards and we give them to ourselves all the time, even though they may not be suitable. Giving yourself a banana split for losing five pounds defeats your purpose. Going to a movie or buying a new tape or CD would be much more satisfying.

The rewards we give our-selves and the enjoyment that comes from reaching our goals are both wonderful pleasures.

JUST GO

"When are you leaving?" "I'm not sure." "Where are you going?" "I don't know."

Have you ever taken a vacation like this? Most of us are so programmed toward specific goals that this would be a very foreign conversation for us. I am the first to agree that if you don't have goals you will become a wandering generality. However, staying on a specific track all the time is like never getting off the freeway.

Be spontaneous once in a while. Take some time, get in the car, and just choose a direction. Get off the freeways; see whom you can meet and what you can find. Be open to ideas and free of time restrictions. Let life progress at its own pace.

Enjoy! Just enjoy.

LETTERS

*S*ome people communicate better by talking with each other. Others need to write things down. I love to visit with my family and friends, but when it comes to feelings, I want to write them down. Maybe that is why I put so much about feelings into my books.

When the mail arrives, if someone has written me a long letter, I will curl up with a cup of hot tea and cherish every word. I read letters over and over and then save them.

Sit down today and put your thoughts and feelings into a long letter to a family member or friend. You will give pleasure to the person receiving the letter, but you also will benefit from the greater feeling of closeness both of you will feel. You might even receive a letter in return.

PINK LEMONADE

*N*ot too many years ago, I worked so hard that I missed summer. I vowed never to do that again.

Summer should be full of laughter and fun. It should be filled with hammocks, pink lemonade, boat rides, fishing poles, fireflies, and picnic ants.

In the summer, I can pack away the treadmill and exercise outside. I can store the winter coat and put on shorts. I can smell the flowers and let the wind blow through my hair.

To me, summer is peace.

Sit back and relax. Pick up that ice-filled glass of pink lemonade and propose a toast with me: "Here's to summer. Here's to peace and joy and pink lemonade."

MEMORY JAR

A memory jar is a place where you store little pieces of paper on which you have written a special thought. It might be a story someone shared with you that made you laugh, or something you did that made someone smile, or something you saw that made you feel warm inside.

The memories in your memory jar might not mean anything to anyone else. They are just yours. They are a special place in your world where you go when you need a little boost for the day.

Make a memory jar and add joy to your day.

TAKE A NAP

We know that napping is good for us; people who take short naps in the early afternoon wake up with reduced stress and increased alertness. In many countries, an afternoon nap is part of everyday life.

So why do I feel guilty when I fall asleep? Why do I deny that I was napping when someone calls and wakes me up? Why does taking a nap make me feel lazy and unproductive?

Maybe I should take a lesson from the many highly productive people who were great nappers, like Winston Churchill and Thomas Edison.

Maybe you should lay this book in your lap right now and trrrrry aaaa snooooooooze . . .

IT'S NEVER TOO LATE

*W*hen author Ann McGee-Cooper was a little girl, she always wanted to tap-dance, but for various reasons she never did. So on her fiftieth birthday, she went out and bought herself a pair of tap shoes and a self-teaching video. (She said she couldn't find a teacher who would take her on.)

To show that it's never too late to learn something new, Ann now tap-dances at the end of her public presentations! She will never make it to Broadway, but she gives it all she has. I think it is a wonderful lesson on fulfilling our heart's desire.

Many of us have things we wish we had learned to do, or maybe we enjoyed doing something long ago and would like to do it again. Why not now?

U R Special

*W*e know that the way we feel about ourselves is very often directly attached to how we look, yet there are thousands of children in the world who have never had anything new to wear. When we feel good about ourselves, we treat other people better, and they usually return the kindness. That is why U R Special Ministries was started. It is a nonprofit organization that provides new clothing (usually handmade) for children who have never had anything new.

This book talks about the little pleasures of life. U R Special Ministries, which provides hundreds of outfits for children three times a year, is one of my greatest pleasures. The children grab those clothes and won't let go of them, even when they need to be altered.

We sometimes become very tired trying to get all those clothes ready, but when a little child looks up at us with big shining eyes and says, "Thank you for my new clothes," that is all it takes. We simply ask, "Where is the sewing machine? I'm ready to go to work again."

Get outside of yourself if you want to know the ultimate pleasure in life. Give to others. Give to a child. There is no better feeling.

DAILY REFRESHMENT

*H*ow do you refresh yourself? What do you do to put yourself back together after a long, hard day at work or with the kids?

Sit perfectly still for fifteen minutes. Restore your mind and body before you make the transition into your next responsibility. It may be the most important fifteen minutes in your day and in the day of the most significant people in your world.

CLOUDS

*A*irplanes and cars. Giraffes, tigers, and lambs. Shoes and flags and faces. They are all there . . . in the clouds.

Remember when you were a kid and didn't have to drive, so you could look out the window? Remember when you had time to lie in the yard and make pictures in the sky? Remember the peace?

The clouds are still there. Don't miss them.

CONGRATULATE YOURSELF

*W*e are not perfect! Whew, isn't that a relief? Because we aren't perfect, we don't do things perfectly all the time. And that is okay.

That doesn't mean we can't congratulate ourselves, and often. For example, my goal when I was writing this book was to write ten pages a day. Not ten perfect pages a day or even ten publishable pages a day, just ten draft pages a day. When those ten pages were completed, I found some way to congratulate myself.

Sometimes we just need to reach around, pat ourselves on the back, and say "You did a great job today." We deserve it.

IMPROMPTU PARTIES

*W*hen you have one of those days filled with deadlines, ringing phones, and confusion, throw a party! One of the best ways to deal with stress is to laugh. Run to the store and pick up a little fruit, some energy drinks, and hats and horns. The party needn't take long, but everyone will laugh and relax, and I guarantee that when you return to work, production levels will increase.

Parties work at home, too. Say that the winter has gone on forever and everyone has cabin fever. Have a "throw away the blues" party. Heat up the house and encourage the guests to wear their summer clothes. Set up a picnic in the middle of the floor. Get into the swing of spring.

Have fun with life. It's not a practice run. It's the real thing.

SAND CASTLES

I was near the ocean recently and had arrived at my destination early enough to drive around a little before dark. As I drove along a beautiful beach, it hit me. Why not stop and build a sand castle?

I did and it was wonderful. I dug in the sand, found an old paper cup, and began my design.

My castle didn't have much discernible shape, but I didn't care. It didn't matter that it was not perfect. I had fun.

FIREWORKS

*F*ireworks light up the sky with the brilliance of light. They seem to symbolize joy and happiness and, yes, freedom. They remind us of the many little moments of pleasure and excitement in our lives.

Impromptu explosions remind us that it's the fireworks in life that make it worth living.

NIGHT SOUNDS

*T*he night has a charm all its own. The mysterious sounds of crickets, frogs, and owls make it a different world.

When I was a child we had no air conditioning. We opened the window instead. So I was used to lying in bed at night and listening to the sounds of the night. I loved them. It was like having the night wrap its arms around me and hold me tight for a long, peaceful rest.

Open your window and listen to these comforting sounds. They are free. They are the little things that matter, the little things that help us keep the big things in perspective.

MASSAGE

A few years ago, for my birthday, my husband gave me a gift certificate for a massage. I had never done such a thing and was not sure I wanted to expose my naked body to someone I had never seen before. (It is bad enough at the doctor's office!) But he convinced me to try it.

It was wonderful! I have never felt so relaxed in all my life. Every muscle had lost its tension and was at ease. In fact, I wondered if I could manage to walk out of the room.

Let me encourage you. If this is one pleasure you have not allowed yourself to experience yet—do it. Find yourself a professional massage therapist and enjoy.

A Flower Garden

My grandmother raised roses. She had roses of every color and size and shape. They were magnificent. Now that I know a little bit about what it takes to raise beautiful roses, they seem even more beautiful to me.

She nurtured those roses every day, and her home was always filled with them. At the time I didn't think much about it, but now I know that she was building good childhood memories for me.

I do a lot of work with at-risk children, some of whom are mistreated and unwanted and know it. Many of them live in urban areas; they have never been in a rose garden or had a grandmother like mine, and I want to weep. I want to take them back to my memories and help them build their own.

I want them to feel safe and secure.

I am grateful that I had a grandmother who loved roses and wanted to share them with me. I am grateful that I have the opportunity to share with these children, and I pray that in some small way I, too, will build happy memories for them.

HERE'S TO MOVIES

*M*ovies are a wonderful form of quick entertainment. You can travel, dream, laugh, or cry. The choice is always yours. I personally like the ones that make me laugh and feel good and happy inside.

Add some variety to your movie-going. See one at six in the morning. Afternoon movies were a habit when I was a kid, but now it seems ridiculous to go to one while the sun is shining. I used to attend midnight sneak previews, but I haven't been to one for years.

If you don't want to go out, rent a movie or tape a TV movie you can't watch when it's on; then have popcorn and movies at home. You can still hold hands on the couch.

That is what is special about "simple" pleasures. They are always our choice.

NOT FISHING

*M*y husband loves to fish and I hate it. But I love to be with him, so I have learned how to not fish.

I'm always happy on the water. I don't particularly like to swim, but I enjoy the peace and the beauty. Lakes are among the most beautiful places I know. I have been on little lakes in Oklahoma, big lakes in Alaska, and the Great Lakes. They all fascinate me.

I can sit on the dock by the lake for hours and stare into the distance. Or ride in a boat, lie back in the sun, drag my hand in the water, and watch the clouds. Or just read.

So we have learned to compromise. Robert gets to fish, I get to be on the water, and we can still be together.

How much better could it possibly get?

JIGSAW PUZZLES

*T*here must be something in human nature that makes us want to fit things together. Look at all the people who build model airplanes or trains or ships. It is quite popular now to build little cities with the greatest detail.

Jigsaw puzzles fascinate me. Frequently, during the holidays, I will put one out on a table and let people work on it when they come by. No one can pass by without trying to add at least one piece.

My problem is that when we get one of these intricate creations put together, I don't want to tear it apart. All that work for nothing! Maybe that is why you can find framed puzzles in my house. They're a visible reminder of the pleasure we had putting them together.

LOOK AROUND YOU

*H*ave you seen the sun set recently? Have you watched the rain run down a windowpane? Have you noticed a rainbow? Have you made time to watch the snow drift through the trees?

If you answered *no* to any of these questions, then you have been too busy. When we get too busy, we forget to look around us. When we get too busy, we forget to enjoy life.

We miss a child's laughter and the gleam in the eye of a loved one. We miss the tulips bursting out of the ground and the tiny leaves growing daily on the trees. We may even miss out on a hug.

Don't miss out on life's simple pleasures.

RITUALS

I guess every family has rituals. Rituals are important. They help us to understand, deep down inside, that we belong.

One of our family's rituals is the way we spend our holidays. As a child, I knew that when it came time to put up the tree at Christmas, Dad and I would decorate it while Mom made hot chocolate. My children knew that their stockings, filled with goodies, would be hanging on the fireplace on Christmas morning, and they would impatiently wait until it was time to open them. Dad no longer trims the tree with me and the children no longer race for the stockings, but the stockings are filled and waiting and the memories are still there. And now we have new rituals.

Jennifer would feel left out if I didn't make her favorite

dishes for holiday dinners. The one year I didn't decorate the house to the hilt, the children noticed. I would feel very strange if they did not help us to put up the big tree in the living room following Thanksgiving dinner.

It is the simple things that become so important. It is not what is in the stockings as much as the fact that they are there. What we eat for holiday dinners is not as important as the fact that we are all together.

Rituals hold us together. Never lose them.

HOMEMADE ICE CREAM

I love ice cream. Though I don't eat it much anymore, it reminds me of happy times in my childhood.

I remember hot summer days when the neighbors would bring their lawn chairs over in the evening to sit and talk in the yard. We kids climbed trees and rode bikes until dark. Often, we made ice cream.

Mom would take the metal can and fill it with fresh milk, sugar, eggs, and vanilla. Dad put it in the wooden bucket, packed it with ice, put a blanket on top, and turned the handle.

Finally the paddle came out, dripping with fresh, rich homemade ice cream. Mom would put it on a plate and we got to eat the ice cream right from the paddle. Ummmm!!

Memories. They just don't get any better.

A SPECIAL CAT

*C*ats are a unique breed. People usually either love them or hate them. My husband is someone who hates cats—all except Taylor. Taylor is different. He was an unexpected blessing in our lives.

Taylor showed up one afternoon, walked into the house, and made himself at home. Within a few days, he had endeared himself to us all.

Maybe your cat is like Taylor. Taylor brings freshness to our lives. He is always there to play with or to love. He helps our house feel more like a home. Having Taylor is a special kind of pleasure.

BOOKS

$\mathcal{Y}$ou can do anything, be anywhere, or become anyone through books. They open up a world we might never be able to touch in any other way. They can make us think, feel, laugh, and cry. They answer our questions and create new ones.

Books are good friends.

THE UNEXPECTED

*S*ome of my most wonderful memories have come from unexpected experiences. I have learned to keep my eyes and ears open for them.

One weekend, I drove with friends to the tiny town of Lajitas on the Mexican border. The town had only one building, an ancient store in the middle of nowhere.

It was hot and we stopped for a cold drink. As I sat down at an old piano, a ragged old man walked up and asked me, "Can you play?" I said, "A little, can you?" He said he did and I asked him to play for us.

The man sat down at that piano and the place became Carnegie Hall. I've never heard such magnificent music. He turned our day into a unique adventure.

Be open. Let life surprise you once in a while.

ANNUAL FRIENDS

*H*ave you ever had friends who were so special that no matter where they lived it was worth it to "make" time to get together once or twice a year? Jim and Jan are like that for us.

When we met, we were instant friends. Robert and Jim love to play golf and Jan and I love to go to arts-and-crafts shows, so we always enjoy our time together. They are special.

When you make connections with people like that, don't lose track of them. These are lifetime friendships. I can see us years from now taking a bus tour to see the fall leaves, because we are too old to drive anymore. I can see us sharing rocking chairs on a front porch. I can see us giving to each other and expecting nothing in return.

That is what friendship is all about.

SMILES

A smile is a pleasure you can give away. I love the bumper sticker that says, "If you see someone without a smile, give them one of yours."

Who knows? You might get one back.

PHOTO OPPORTUNITIES

*W*e were sitting on the beach one day in Mexico, watching the tourists parasailing out over the ocean. I said, "That looks like so much fun." Robert said, "Yes, I've always wanted to do it." I replied, "Then do it."

Much to my astonishment, he did. I am not sure who had the most fun, Robert parasailing or me taking pictures.

It was fabulous! Just to watch them get ready was worth the trip. An elderly man with amazing strength and stamina swam way out into the ocean to get the rope to attach to the harness and the boat. The driver put the harness on Robert and gave him all sorts of directions about which rope to pull when and what all their signals meant. Then off he went!

I was clicking pictures as fast as I could. I didn't want to miss a moment of the lift-off or the rise up over the ocean and across the mountain. Then he started back, and I was determined to capture every moment so we could enjoy forever his descent and the joy on his face as he touched down.

At that moment, I ran out of film.

Life's little pleasures. If you're out of film, just keep them in your mind's eye.

TALENTS

*E*xploring our talents can be a great source of pleasure, for us and for others.

I love to sew. I love the creativity of fitting pieces together to create a whole. I sew for myself and for others, but mainly because I enjoy it. I think we need to do things we enjoy for their own sake.

My neighbor works in his yard all the time. It is beautiful. You can tell from the way he works that he is doing it because he loves it.

What are your talents? Maybe you can paint or write. Maybe your talent is creating a delicious meal, or building dollhouses, or being a friend.

Do what you love. Make time in your life for enhancing your talents. You will find a great source of pleasure when you nurture them.

GAMES

*G*ames can be a wonderful way to enjoy a cold winter afternoon or share time with friends and family.

My family has spent many hours playing Monopoly and we have learned a lot about each other through a surprisingly revealing game called Uno. On trips, we always carry a deck of cards for a gin match on an airplane or in a hotel room.

Our newest challenge is computer games. When our kids come home, we get together for Family Feud on the computer.

A game doesn't have to be complicated or expensive to be fun. Think about children playing jacks or marbles or checkers or Go Fish.

Games are a way of sharing, and what is more fun than sharing time, ideas, and laughter with those you love?

YOU GOTTA LAUGH

*M*y mom and dad had been married over sixty-one years when we lost my dad. A couple of days later my mom and I were at the funeral home when I said, "Mom, my husband reminds me that when we die and go to heaven, we can't be married to the same person we are married to on earth. I think that is very sad. If I can't be married to Robert in heaven, it just won't be heaven to me."

My mom looked at my dad for a moment and then said, "Well, I guess *we'll* just have to shack up."

What a joy to share laughter with those you love. It is how we share our hearts.

Home Beautiful

I visited a gorgeous home recently. Everything matched perfectly and it looked like a *House Beautiful* ad. I wondered why my home didn't look like that. Something was missing.

As I began to study our home, I saw the difference. In my friend's home, all the paintings had been bought to match the decor. Mine were not.

One of mine came from Boston during the Bicentennial, where we saw a woman painting marvelous watercolors of the tall ships. That little rabbit came from a crafts show in Arkansas. And the embossed hearts—well, they just made me feel good inside.

My home will never make a *House Beautiful* ad, but it is a "home beautiful" to us.

ONLY A MOMENT

*H*e came running down the hall calling out his name for me: "MeMe, MeMe!" He knew I was leaving on a trip, and he thought I had left without saying good-bye.

I scooped him up in my arms and assured him that I would never leave without saying good-bye. I kissed his tears and hugged away his fears.

It took only a moment. Only a moment to kiss away the tears. Only a moment to know how much I was loved and needed. What a joy.

INSPIRATION

*W*hen I was eighteen, I moved to Colorado and learned how to ski. On my first trip up the chairlift, I was very frightened. An elderly gentleman was sitting next to me. He was in his eighties and this was his first trip up the ski slope, too. He was elated. I was terrified.

He jumped off the chairlift and glided down the mountain. I never saw him again, and he never knew that he was one of the great inspirations of my life. I looked at him and thought, "I can do it, too. And if I can't, I am still going to try."

I have thought about my fellow skier during every challenge in my life. He became a source of courage to me and never knew it. How often have we had the pleasure of being an inspiration to someone? Maybe we will today.

PAJAMA DAY

*M*y friend Julie and her family have a wonderful custom. They have what they call "Pajama Day."

Periodically, they take a day off, the whole family stays at home, and they spend the entire day in their pajamas. They eat when they want to. They sleep when they feel like it. They read, talk, watch movies, and play games.

Isn't it interesting how we program ourselves to spend our days in certain ways? Maybe it's time for a change. Maybe it's time for a Pajama Day.

LOVE WITH YOUR SENSES

*L*ove one another
with all your senses:
With your eyes . . . let
them shine at the one you love.

With your ears . . . really
listen to what others say. Listening says they are important to
your world.

With your touch . . . we
thrive on the touch of others.
Don't pass up a hug.

With your scent . . . wear a
favorite cologne. Let that scent
be yours and make memories.

With your taste . . . savor
the moments. Make them as
real in your memory's eye as the
taste of your favorite food.

And the sixth sense is—
intuition. Be intuitive to others'
needs. Do it before they ask.
Say it before they wish. Be there
before they long for you.

Love comes back sixfold.

LAUGHING FRIENDS

riends are one of the great blessings of life. They are there when you need them. They listen and share and care, and if they have to, they step on your toes to help you stay on target. And some are laughing friends.

Our laughing friends are Virgil and Gwen. We have known them most of our lives and we know a lot about each other. Maybe that is why it is so easy to laugh together. They know why we do all the weird things that we do.

When times get challenging, we call Virgil and Gwen. We live ninety miles apart now, but that doesn't matter. We make arrangements to meet and we have dinner and laugh. They are so easy to laugh with. That makes them very precious to us.

PLACES YOU LOVE

*W*hat are your favorite places? What do you find there? Is it the people who intrigue you or the architecture? Maybe it's the culture or the history. Perhaps you like small towns where everyone knows everyone else, or you may prefer a metropolitan atmosphere. Maybe your favorite places are old haunts or the neighborhood where you grew up.

The places you love are those where you find your own special kind of pleasure. They make you feel good inside. They make you feel at home.

INNER PEACE

*H*e called just to say hello. That wasn't unusual. Her dad frequently did that just before he left on a trip. They chatted briefly and just before she hung up she said, "Remember, Dad, I love you."

Later that day, his car crossed a median and crashed. It was over in a matter of seconds. She never saw him alive again.

"But I said 'I love you,'" she told me. "The last thing I said to my dad was 'I love you.' I didn't know that it would be our last conversation. I'm so glad I did that."

Sometimes the greatest pleasure we have is inner peace. The knowledge that we did something right this time. That we have no regrets.

WILDFLOWERS

*F*lowers make the world a more beautiful place to live.

I especially enjoy wildflowers. I love driving through Texas and seeing fields of bluebonnets. I am very grateful to Lady Bird Johnson for encouraging everyone to throw a handful of wildflower seeds on vacant lots and along the roadways. In almost every state, you can see the natural beauty of wildflowers just by driving down the highways.

My first trip to Seattle was a special joy because wildflowers were everywhere. I had never been to a city that had flowers growing in the alleys. What a beautiful place!

Do your city a favor. Buy a package of wildflower seeds and cast them in a vacant lot. Nature will do the rest.

THAT SPECIAL TOUCH

*D*oes the most significant person in your world touch you in a very special way? Is there a certain look that only you recognize? Does he or she do something that triggers special memories for you?

Wonderful, isn't it? When my husband touches my back in a certain way, I feel that I am an important part of our little world. I love the way his eyes glisten when he glances my way. Just a word or touch can bring a sparkle to the dreariest day.

When Robert calls me, he always says, "Hello, fantastic person. I love you." If I ever picked up the phone and didn't hear that, my world would be a much sadder place. Those six words make my day. They always have and I hope they always will.

95

BEGINNERS' EYES

*W*hen I was younger, there was not much I would not try. This gave me some wonderful experiences. One of those was deep-sea diving.

A group of us took a diving trip to a little island off the coast of Florida. I was the least experienced diver, so I decided to stay close to the boat while the others dove farther out. It turned out that I was the most fortunate.

That night, at dinner, my stories got the most attention. I told them about some objects like anchors I saw resting against the coral and about other objects I had found on the bottom that looked like barrels. It turned out that I had discovered a ship that had been wrecked in the 1800s!

We dove down to the shipwreck for three days and

brought back coins, crystal, and bottles. What an experience! And all because I was so new at what I was doing that I was fascinated by the simplest things I saw.

Being a beginner helped me see things I might not ever have noticed. Maybe we all need to take the time to see the beautiful things around us through the eyes of a beginner.

THE SEASONS

I grew up in West Texas, where we had two seasons: mild summer and hot summer. You can imagine my total amazement when I moved to Colorado and found four magnificent seasons.

Spring's flowers and the trees covered with tiny green leaves are replaced by summer's meadows, ready for picnics, and brooks running with ice-cold water from the mountain snows.

The fall is filled with deep colors—gold and red and wine. And the winter—ah, the picture-perfect, snow-covered mountains and laughing children everywhere throwing snowballs.

I love West Texas. The people are wonderful. It is my home. But the four seasons were an addition to my life that nothing will ever replace.

What a beautiful world we live in!

BICYCLING

icycling is a wonderful way of taking the time to enjoy the little pleasures of life. You can hear the birds sing. You can smell the flowers. You can enjoy the breeze blowing through your hair. You can talk with a friend.

I guess I am just a kid at heart. I remember the hours I spent riding around my neighborhood when I was a child and I long to buy a new bike and recapture those joyful feelings once again.

COLLECTIONS

*M*y friends and family all have collections—angels, bells, ceramic pigs, nutcrackers, unicorns. I love adding to their collections and knowing that I have pleased them. I am a passionate collector of books. I enjoy both collecting them and using them.

Buttons, baseball cards, books, stamps, seashells, rocks, antique china, postcards . . . Collect and surround yourself with the things you love.

PEOPLE WATCHING

*A*re you a people watcher? Do you ever sit in a restaurant or on a bench in the mall and make up stories about the people you see? Look. There is a happy family. Oh, the blonde doesn't belong. See how they are trying to please her? She must be visiting.

I bet that person works with his hands. Look at them! They are so strong. He must be very creative. He probably doesn't just lay bricks; he is the one who builds cathedrals.

People are so special in their own delightfully unique way. They have challenges and joys and happinesses, and seeing them and imagining who they are makes me feel a part of life. How wonderful.

A ROARING FIRE

*S*ome of my most
precious memories are
of the wonderful but rare times I
get to build a roaring fire in the
fireplace and curl up with a
good book for a long, peaceful
evening. There is something
about the fire that mesmerizes
me. It makes me feel calm and
collected inside.

I love a roaring fire. My
husband doesn't understand. He
says that we don't have to use
the fireplace—we have central
heat. Personally, I would turn
up the air conditioning and
light a fire even in July.

THE SECOND MILE

here is a scripture that encourages us to go the second mile with others, to do more than is expected of us, to give more than we have to, to be more than is required.

I heard a wonderful presentation recently where that second mile was called the "love mile." You give extra time and money and effort not because you have to, but because you love—because you care. What a nice way to live!

I know people like that. They always go out of their way for others. When they say "Call me if you need anything," they really mean it. They are the first ones there when something happens, and they always seem to know what to do. They don't wait to be asked; they volunteer. These people are the "love milers." They do what needs to be done . . . and then some.

We are richly blessed when we have people like that in our world. And they are everywhere. If you look around, you will see them, but you have to look. They are not usually the people making the headlines.

You will find them in the kitchen washing dishes after a wedding or a funeral. They bring in a meal or mow the lawn for the family expecting triplets. They offer to pick up some of your workload when they know you sat up all night with a sick loved one. They make the time to listen when you need someone to talk to, even though they are probably the busiest people on earth.

Who are these second milers—these people who give and give, and then some? They are called friends.

It isn't
the great big pleasures
that count the most;
it's making a great deal
out of the little ones.

—JEAN WEBSTER,
DADDY LONG-LEGS

ACKNOWLEDGMENTS

The writing of this book could never have been accomplished without the support of my family. My husband, Robert, is the one who gives me that daily encouragement that we all need. My daughters, my mother, and my mother-in-love are the ones who help when time gets tight and make it possible for me to maintain my schedule. Without my immediate and extended family, life would not be nearly as pleasurable.

A special thanks goes to the wonderful and talented people who made time to review and comment on the final manuscript. I appreciate your encouraging words. You are special!

Judith Briles
Barbara Fielder
Barbara Johnson
Marty Johnson
Ann McGee-Cooper
Naomi Rhode

Rena Tarbet
Brian Tracy
Virgil Trout
Marilyn Van Derbur
Joanne Wallace

A number of helpful people made time to read early drafts of the manuscript. Their constructive comments made all the difference. Thanks so much to:

Osalee Banzett
Shelly Beaird
Catherine H. Brown

Alline Chandler
Norma Church
Carol Clark

Kay Coldiron
Bertha Cruz-Gaede
Claudette Dills
Verner R. Ekstrom
Stormy Erhardt
Donna Fisher
Georgia M. Gaalaas
Doris Harty
Jerre Heaton
Elise Hensley
Julie Herbison
Gary John
Kristine Kostoff
Carol Larimore
Heather Lopez-Cepero
Phyllis McConnell
Lois M. Mitchell

Kathy Monte
Glorianne Perrizo
Debbie Price
Rachel Redmon
Laura Renshaw
Anthony Renzi
Marcia Ross
Mary Ann Ross
Linda Ryncavage
Beth Sledge
Sherry Sprague
Victoria Stephen
Belvia Walls
Florence Watson
Wilma Willbanks
Sheenia Williams-Wesley

Without the expert guidance of the Bard &
Stephen team, this book would not have become
a reality. Ray Bard and Leslie Stephen skillfully
guided the book to completion in such a kind and
thoughtful manner. I thank you for your patience
and expertise. Helen Hyams is more than just a
good editor. She even says nice things to me in
the process. Thanks, Helen, I love it. And to
Suzanne Pustejovsky for her talent in design, a
special thanks. You are essential to our success.

You are all very special.

U R Special Ministries

U R Special Ministries, Inc., is a nonprofit program that helps at-risk children between the ages of three and ten to feel important by providing them with new clothing. These children may never have had anything new to wear.

There is a direct connection between the way people look and how they feel about who they are. This program is designed to help young people begin their growth toward a positive future. Our motto is "Building self-esteem through love."

Through the ministry, we tell precious little children every day how special they are. We put the label "U R SPECIAL" on each outfit, feeling that if the youngsters hear and see this phrase enough, they will believe it. And if they believe it, we can make a difference in their lives.

U R Special Ministries is not affiliated with any church, although many church groups are involved in sewing, knitting, and crocheting garments. At present, groups and individuals from eight states provide clothing, along with home economics classes and vocational-technical schools all over Oklahoma.

If you would like more information on this group or want to help, please write or call:

U R Special Ministries, Inc.
P.O. Box 32762
Oklahoma City, OK 73123
405-478-1011

THE DONNA WATSON GROUP

The mission of The Donna Watson Group is to help people discover their own power and energy. Dr. Watson's presentations, whether keynote speeches or information-packed seminars, are known for their practical techniques and strategies. Her warm and witty style encourages people to think and grow—and to feel good about themselves.

Thousands of people from all types and sizes of organizations—including Fortune 500 corporations, growing companies, government agencies, and associations—have attended Donna's seminars. They include American Floral Service, General Motors, Emory University, International Paper, Kroger Foods, Motorola, Shawnee Indian Health Center, Tenneco, and the U.S. Marine Corps.

Donna's undergraduate degree is in education and her MBA and Ph.D. degrees are in management. Her Ph.D. dissertation focused on stress management. In addition to authoring *101 Simple Ways to Be Good to Yourself* and *101 Ways to Enjoy Life's Simple Pleasures,* Donna has recorded two six-tape albums, *Let Go and Live* on stress and self-esteem and *Winning Against Stress* on stress management.

For information about the services of The Donna Watson Group, call:

The Donna Watson Group
405-478-1011

ORDER FORM

Quantity	Material	Total
	101 Ways to Enjoy Life's Simple Pleasures	
_____	Paperback edition, 128 pages, $7.95	_____
_____	Hardcover edition, 128 pages, $12.95	_____
	101 Simple Ways to Be Good to Yourself	
_____	Paperback edition, 128 pages, $7.95	_____
_____	Hardcover edition, 128 pages, $12.95	_____
_____	*Let Go and Live* Six-tape album on self-esteem and stress management, $46.95	_____
_____	*Winning Against Stress* Six-tape album on stress management with 30-page workbook, $54.95	_____
	Sales tax (Texas residents only)	_____
	Shipping and handling ($2.00 for first book, $1.00 per book thereafter)	_____
	TOTAL	_____

**Quantity Discounts
are available.
1-800-945-3132**

☐ Please contact me about your workshops, presentations, and corporate seminars

Name _____

Organization _____

Address _____

City _____ State _____ Zip _____

Telephone (_____) _____

Please check one:
☐ MasterCard   ☐ VISA   Exp. Date _____

Card Number _____

Signature _____